The Basics of Essay Writing

Essay writing is at the heart of education. Students at every level need to be able to write clear and well-organised essays whether in the form of assignments, dissertations or examination answers. In this handy guidebook bestselling author Nigel Warburton provides all the advice you need to develop your academic writing skills and improve your marks.

The book opens with a discussion of why essay writing matters, and proceeds in a straightforward style through the basics of the craft. Topics covered include:

- Getting started
- Making a case
- Examination essays
- Achieving clarity

Written in the author's accomplished, student-friendly style, *The Basics of Essay Writing* is full of practical tips and guidance. Students of all ages and in every subject area will find it indispensable.

Nigel Warburton is Senior Lecturer at The Open University where he chairs the highly successful *Start Writing* courses. His previous books include *Philosophy: The Basics* (4th edition), *Thinking from A to Z* (2nd edition), *Philosophy: The Classics* (3rd edition) and *Philosophy: The Essential Study Guide*, all published by Routledge.

NIGEL WARBURTON

The Basics of Essay Writing

Routledge
Taylor & Francis Group

LONDON AND NEW YORK

First published 2006 by Routledge
2 Park Square, Milton Park, Abingdon, Oxon, OX14 4RN

Simultaneously published in the USA and Canada
by Routledge
270 Madison Ave, New York NY 10016

Routledge is an imprint of the Taylor & Francis Group

Transferred to Digital Printing 2007

© 2006 Nigel Warburton

Typeset in Rotis by Keystroke, Jacaranda Lodge, Wolverhampton

British Library Cataloguing in Publication Data
A catalogue record for this book is available from the British Library

Library of Congress Cataloging in Publication Data
Warburton, Nigel, 1962–
The basics of essay writing/Nigel Warburton
     p. cm.
Includes bibliographical references.
ISBN 0-415-23999-0 (alk. paper)–ISBN 0-415-24000-X (pbk: alk.
paper). 1. English language–Composition and exercises–Study
and teaching (Secondary)   2. Report writing–Study and Teaching
(Secondary)   I. Title.
LB1631. W246   2006
808'.042'0712–dc22
2005023377

ISBN10: 0-415-23999-0 (hbk)
ISBN10: 0-415-24000-X (pbk)

ISBN13: 9-78-0-415-23999-8 (hbk)
ISBN13: 9-78-0-415-24000-0 (pbk)

Contents

Contents

Contents

Acknowledgements

I am extremely grateful to my agent Caroline Dawnay at pfd for suggesting that I write this book, and to my editor at Taylor & Francis, Philip Mudd. I am also grateful for comments on the draft from publisher's readers, and from Anna Motz, Lucy Thorp, and Peter Harrison. Many students at various universities and colleges have contributed to my understanding of the basics of essay writing without realising it. Thanks to them too.

Nigel Warburton
Oxford 2005

Introduction

How to use this book

This book is for anyone who has to write essays. It covers the basics of the craft. Most people worry about writing essays, but if you have a reasonable grasp of your subject and the will-power to practise writing, you can make significant improvements very quickly. My aim has been to focus on what can really make a difference. Get the basics right and you can improve in your next essay. Don't feel obliged to read the book from cover to cover. Dip into it. Find strategies that work for you.

Remember, though, that reading this book shouldn't be an alternative to writing. If you want to improve, then you need to *write*, not just read about writing. Otherwise, you will be like someone learning the theory of swimming but never dipping a toe in the water. There is no adequate substitute for learning through *doing*. One of the toughest aspects of essay writing is getting started. But writing won't be enough: you need to be able to recognise your own strengths and weaknesses, and adapt your style accordingly. You will need to work on *improving* your writing, not just doing more of it. It isn't the number of hours that you practise that matters; it is the quality of your practice that will determine what you achieve. This book should help you by providing a guide for self-improvement.

It is little use having an in-depth knowledge of your chosen subject if you lack the basic skills of written communication. But just a few hours of focused work could set you on the road to academic success. Good luck.

Key points

- Practise essay writing: don't just read about it.
- The quality of practice is more important than the quantity.

1
What's the Point?

Writing essays

Essay writing is at the heart of education. Whatever you study, at some point you will be asked to write an essay. And if you aren't, then you probably won't ever weave together the different strands of what you've learnt. In humanities subjects – Literature, History, Philosophy and so on – students are judged on their essays. If you can't write good essays, particularly under exam conditions, then you will never succeed in these areas. Some students fail to achieve their potential simply because they don't understand the basic principles of essay writing. They can be convincing in discussion and know the subject well, but when it comes to writing an essay they fall apart. *Talking* about what you know isn't enough (though it may be an important part of the learning process): you need to be able to make a clear and well-argued case in writing, based on appropriate research. This remains the most effective way to demonstrate your understanding of your subject and your ability to use what you know.

Many students, even those studying practice-based subjects, such as Fine Art or Photography, also have to write a dissertation. So do students in the sciences and social sciences. This can be daunting if you are not used to writing. But it needn't be. The same principles of good essay writing apply to longer pieces of work. And these principles can be learnt. The process of putting together a coherent essay, short or long, is not a mystery, nor is it particularly complicated: you just have to build a good case for your conclusion and structure your whole essay around that aim.

Some people seem to have natural writing talent: they can write well without putting much effort or thought into the process. But most of us have to devote time and energy to this activity. Nearly everyone can make significant improvements. Writing skills are transferable, so progress here can have an impact on your whole academic career. The skills of clear writing, and of developing and supporting an argument, are fundamental to all non-fiction writing and will probably be relevant to your professional life after college. If you turn to creative writing, many of the principles apply there too. But beyond that, writing can be a pleasure, particularly when you are in the flow of it, when it suddenly seems simple and all the ideas fit together almost by themselves.

Writing is thinking

Don't make the mistake of thinking of an essay as copying out something you've already thought through in great detail. Some people assume they can't begin to write until they have an almost perfect essay worked out in their head, or at least a sentence-by-sentence essay plan. This is usually a mistake. For most of us, writing an essay is not a matter of listening to an internal voice dictating a pre-imagined essay. Getting down to writing is very important. It is often in the act of writing that the subject comes into focus for the first time. I've had the experience in the middle of an examination of suddenly understanding the connections between different parts of a syllabus in a way that eluded me throughout my revision. Writing is a kind of thinking.

When you have to defend a position in writing, to argue using your own examples, or to reason to a conclusion drawing only on relevant material, then you are forced to grapple with your subject in a new way. Don't be tempted to put it off for too long. Not that planning is a bad idea. Most writers make at least sketchy plans before starting to write – a few headings, a few keywords, some arrows, perhaps, linking ideas, and a conclusion. Think of the plan as part of the writing, though, not as something separate from the writing process.

What begins as vague and unfocused gradually emerges as sharp and clear. Or at least that's what it should feel like if you've got into the flow of planning. As you write, you should start to see where you need to do further research before you can say anything that is interesting, accurate and true. It really does make sense to say that you may not know what you think about the topic until you have tried to write about it.

Cultivate good habits

Skills are built on good habits. Habits are patterns of behaviour that you don't need to think about, usually because you've practised them many times before. Once you've got into a good habit, life gets easier. But getting to that stage usually requires self-discipline. There are no guaranteed rewards for practising something badly. Repeating bad habits over and over only makes the habits harder to break. But even a few minutes a day of the right kind of practice can transform your ability. The secret of effective practice is to practise the right things and practise them well: you won't be rewarded in proportion to the hours you put in. You might even reinforce bad habits; high-quality practice, however, always brings about improvement.

If you want to play a musical instrument, you will have to learn the basics and practise them until you don't need to think about them. Then you can concentrate on the structure and interpretation of the music and stop worrying about where to place your fingers. This is true for even the most talented musicians. The same holds for sports. When you see someone who kicks a football without any effort, or is a graceful swimmer or dancer, you can be sure that they have put in many hours of practice to achieve this. Some people start with natural advantages; but we can all progress. If you want to play football for your country or win a major tennis championship, you will have to have a combination of in-born talent and a willingness to work on basic and advanced skills. Essay writing is no different in this respect. Learning to write well involves developing good habits until you no longer need to think about them. The best writers have natural advantages, but if you can read and understand this book, you can certainly bring your writing to a level adequate for university study.

At first you might find it tedious to be considering some of the aspects of essay writing that I cover here. You might even feel that you know all about the basics of essay writing already. Perhaps you do. If so, you don't need this book. But most writers have areas they can improve, and following the guidelines given here could save you many hours of wasted effort. By the end of this book I hope you will recognise that good habits and solid basic skills are the keys that will unlock your potential.

Remember that no one writes perfect essays. Nor is there a single right way to answer any essay question. There is always room for improvement; even the most brilliant writers can improve. You are reading this book, so presumably you feel that you need to work on some aspect of your own writing (unless someone forced you to read it 'for your own good'). Even a small improvement here can have an impact on the grades you receive; it can also greatly enhance your enjoyment of the process. It is very satisfying to produce a well-crafted piece of writing, both because it makes sense of the subject matter, and also because of the pleasure of putting words together in a skilful and creative way. Your best hope of achieving this pleasure is to cultivate good writing habits.

Key points

- Essay writing is at the heart of most academic study.
- Writing is a kind of thinking.
- It is important to form good writing habits.
- The best way to improve is to put in high-quality practice.

2
Start writing

Overcoming psychological obstacles

Writing is a strange activity. If you have an essay to write, it is amazing how easy it is to find other things to do. Writer's block – a total inability to write anything at all – is very rare. But the urge to do something other than write whenever you have writing to do is extremely common. Give someone an essay to write, and suddenly they will remember a list of urgent chores they have to perform before they get started on it. They might 'need' to eat or drink, tidy their desk, or go to the library, go shopping, do the washing up, or surf the Internet for suitable materials. As I'm writing this, I'm feeling a very strong desire to have a nap or at least to go and get myself a coffee to give myself more energy. But I know that this is largely my mind's bid to get me to do something else – almost anything else – rather than write. Luckily I've made it to my word processor, and the words have started to come. But if I'd fallen asleep I would have taken a lot longer to get started.

> It is important to have a way worked out to begin your writing; otherwise, washing the dishes becomes the most important thing on earth – anything that will divert you from writing. Finally, one just has to shut up, sit down, and write.
>
> (Natalie Goldberg, 1998, p. 43)

Professional writers are well aware of their own avoidance strategies, and of those urges to do something – anything – other than write. But these urges aren't always excuses. Perhaps you do genuinely need to do some of these other things. For instance, to write well I know that I need energy. If I just took that nap now, perhaps I'd write much better. There is a whole series of books that tell business people they need to take a 'power nap', the short sleep in the middle of the day that refreshes you and allows you to return to your work with a new vigour. It may be true that you need to do more research before you write that final version of your essay. However, the skill you need to acquire is the skill of beginning: the skill of getting to your desk, or wherever you work, and making a start. What I mean by this is that you should make sure that you at least begin to plan and write your essay. You should get in front of your computer screen or blank page of paper and make the first moves even if you feel that there are many other things you also suddenly need to do. Once you've started the process, writing usually gets much easier and you may find your tiredness evaporating and your urge to do all those other things diminishing.

For some reason, once you recognise the existence of this pattern of writing-avoidance, it is much easier to find strategies for getting down to work. Also, once you have something on paper or on the screen – even just a few words – everything starts to become more manageable. The task seems less daunting.

Try some of these strategies and see what works for you. Give yourself rewards. Start with small, achievable goals, like writing for ten minutes or completing a paragraph, and then have a cup of coffee, a snack or a break. Perhaps play music while you work; use headphones if you are likely to disturb other people. It is completely up to you to decide what to play, but one option is to listen to the same music whenever you write so that it works at the level of a psychological association. Another is to play whatever appeals to you at the time, so that you associate writing with pleasure. This is also a good way of reducing the effect of irritating noises from outside. If you are feeling sluggish, play music that energises you; if you are stressed, choose something more relaxing. I wouldn't recommend listening to a radio station or anything else that is talk based. It is probably too easy to be distracted from the words you are writing when you are listening to someone speaking. Don't believe teachers who say 'You can't possibly write with your headphones on': it's just not true – indeed, some people write better like that. One of the best strategies is to listen to music you know well: that way you are less likely to be distracted by what you hear. The only worry is that if you become too dependent on music you might have difficulty writing under examination conditions, or in libraries or wherever it is difficult or forbidden to listen to music.

Here's another strategy from a highly respected teacher of creative writing:

> Teach yourself as soon as possible to work the moment you sit down to a machine, or settle yourself with pad and pencil. If you find yourself dreaming there, or biting your pencil end, get up and go to the farthest corner of the room. Stay there while you are getting up steam. When you have your first sentence ready, go back to your tools. If you steadily refuse to lose yourself in reverie at your worktable, you will be rewarded by finding that merely taking your seat there will be enough to make your writing flow.
>
> (Dorothea Brande, 1983, p. 161)

Avoid the weight of unfinished business

A good reason for getting down to writing as soon as possible is that having an unfinished assignment hanging over you can have an unpleasant effect on most aspects of your life. Poor time management is a major source of stress and anxiety. Students who lurch from one essay crisis to another usually feel guilty, sleep badly (because they stay up very late trying to meet deadlines) and have a nagging sense that they really should be getting down to work. Lack of sleep can impact on everything you do from study to social life. Unfortunately, good intentions here aren't enough: you need to do the work to get out of this spiral. Remember that getting a few words down on paper may be enough to break that downward momentum.

Do something rather than nothing

A good strategy for completing a large task, such as writing an extended essay or dissertation, is to break it down into smaller, manageable tasks. Plan and write a particular paragraph or section rather than taking on the whole project in one go. Each of these shorter sections should be relatively simple to complete. Don't be too ambitious at first. Achieving a modest goal is far better than setting yourself targets that you may never achieve. It is very satisfying to finish a short, well-crafted paragraph. Once you've started writing something, you will probably find that you want to continue on to the next paragraph and the next. If you find it difficult to write the first paragraph, select one part of the way through the essay that you know you *can* write, and write that one instead. Or write the concluding sentence of the whole essay and work back from that. The important thing is to get started. If you can't bring yourself to write complete sentences, jot down a few headings. But write something.

Customise your approach

Writing is a skill that is closely linked to the kind of person you are. You need to find what works best for you, not simply try to adopt a way of working that suits someone else. You can of course learn from other people's experiences and from other people's writing, but you will need to adapt what you learn to the kind of writer you are capable of becoming. When a tutor sets an essay question, he or she does not have in mind one perfect essay that everyone ought to try very hard to write. There are usually many excellent ways of answering the same question. What you as an essay writer need to develop is a style of writing and an approach to writing that allows you to succeed within the limits of the particular course you are studying. Eventually this way of writing will be quite natural for you. At first, however, you may find that you need to concentrate on the style, rather as when you first learnt to ride a bicycle. Don't be disconcerted by this; swift improvement in essay writing is possible. What you have to avoid is lapsing into old bad habits just because they are easy.

Take breaks

There is no need to work relentlessly until your head begins to nod and you eventually fall asleep at your desk. What will that achieve? Most people are only capable of writing when they are reasonably alert. Taking short breaks is important. It is a good idea to stand up and stretch from time to time; otherwise, you run the risk of tension building up in your muscles without your realising it. A writing session with short breaks every forty minutes or so will be far more productive than grinding on for several hours without a break at all.

Remember that you won't be judged on the number of hours you spend trying to write, but by what you produce. You could spend five hours or five minutes on a paragraph, but what matters is the quality of your writing and argument, not your investment of time and intellectual energy. When you do take a break, as you should, make sure you actually get back to your desk afterwards. Watch out for those 'must do' distractions. When you take a break, look at the clock and decide on a time to start writing again. Stick to that time.

Less than perfect can be good enough

One common problem is that students set their own standards so high that they are always disappointed with what they produce. If you are a perfectionist you will never finish anything because you will always be able to find fault with every sentence that you write, and probably will feel the urge to go back and improve it before moving on to the next sentence. If you begin writing believing that what you write in your first draft will be more or less perfect, then you are unlikely to get very far with the draft. This kind of perfectionism is self-defeating.

You need to recognise that an essay, and particularly at the draft stage, should only be above a threshold: it should be *good enough*. Striving after perfection in the early stages of any writing is counter-productive; it can block the flow completely. *Don't get too critical too soon.* Once you have managed a first draft on paper, *that* is the time to eliminate as many of the minor flaws as possible. By then you should be working on producing the best possible essay you can within your time and energy constraints; however, at an earlier stage, your aim should simply be to get a reasonably coherent draft written all the way through to its conclusion.

Key points

- Everyone finds excuses not to write.
- Putting off essay writing can ruin your social life.
- Writing just a few words can get you started.
- Find writing strategies that work for you.
- Take breaks, but get back to work too.
- Don't aim for a perfect essay: it only has to be good enough.

3
Answer the question

Question: How many surrealists does it take to change a light
bulb?
Answer: a fish.

The worst mistake

*The worst mistake you can make in essay writing is failing to answer
the question asked.* Stop and reread this last sentence. It is a fairly
obvious point, but if you don't grasp it, you are unlikely to succeed
academically. If there is the slightest chance that you will forget
this basic principle, write it out on a large piece of paper and pin
it to your noticeboard, or in front of wherever you work. Most
students who don't answer the question aren't aware that they
haven't answered it. A strict marker may fail your essay completely,
no matter how good it is in itself, if it doesn't directly address the
particular question asked. It is not enough to discuss a topic that
relates to the one in the question. You must answer *the very question
set.* 'Am I really answering the question?' should echo in your
head all the time you are writing, and particularly when you are
beginning a new paragraph or writing your conclusion. Eloquent
digressions are a waste of ink. Never let the marker or examiner
think 'Yes . . . but *so what?*' Answer the question.

Direct questions

If you are attempting to answer a direct question, you should give a direct answer. So, for example, if you are asked 'What is the dramatic function of the porter's scene in Shakespeare's play *Macbeth*?', your answer should include a very clear direct answer about the scene's dramatic function. If you are asked 'Does the porter's scene in *Macbeth* achieve a heightening or a lessening of tension in the play?', then be sure to demonstrate which of these two options you want to defend (assuming your answer isn't 'neither' or 'both'). Direct questions give you a focus for your concluding paragraph: that paragraph should address what has been asked head-on, as, in many cases, should your opening paragraph.

Instruction words

Essay questions or assignment titles usually contain instruction words such as '*discuss*', '*summarise*' or '*criticise*'. You should pay particular attention to these, otherwise you risk not answering the question set. It is worth underlining or circling the key instruction word to remind you to focus on it. I've listed some of them below, together with brief suggestions about what they are instructing you to do. You should, however, always think about the instruction words in their actual context. Some of my comments about the words listed below may not be relevant to the context of the question you are attempting; they are just there as broad guidelines.

analyse: Analysis is usually a matter of taking things apart to see how the different parts contribute to the whole.

assess: The crucial idea here is that you make some kind of value judgement about the matter. In other words, this instruction tells you very clearly that the examiner/marker wants you to come to a conclusion about the view being discussed.

classify: Classification is about putting things into the correct classes.

comment on: This instruction is usually followed by an idea, theory or quotation. You are invited to make critical judgements about this.

compare and contrast: An invitation for you to show both what is similar and what is dissimilar about the explanations/accounts or whatever is under discussion. Be sure both to compare *and* to contrast.

critically discuss: A critical discussion involves engaging with the ideas discussed, not just summarising them.

define: The principal meaning of this instruction is to give a clear definition of something. This typically involves specifying the limits within which something has to fall for it to be that kind of thing.

describe: An opportunity for you to give an account, perhaps a narrative, that is relatively free from critical judgements.

detail: An invitation to provide another kind of description, in this case emphasising the component parts.

discuss: A fairly open-ended invitation to engage critically with the subject.

Answer the question

evaluate: Explain the relative worth of the idea or account, providing justification for your conclusion.

explain: Spell out as if to an intelligent but relatively uninformed person.

illustrate: Provide examples or instances that illuminate the points under discussion.

interpret: Give a plausible account of the data, drawing conclusions from the evidence you have been given.

justify: Provide the evidence and arguments that support the conclusion given.

outline: Give a clear summary, but don't go into too much detail.

refute: Provide the evidence and arguments against the position given and show how a different conclusion follows.

relate: Show the connections between.

review: Summarise and assess.

sketch: Give a clear overview of the main features without going into too much detail.

state: Spell out.

summarise: Select the main features and describe them clearly in your own words.

trace: Show how a particular idea or event was caused by or evolved from earlier ones.

Key points

- The worst mistake you can make is not answering the question.
- Answer direct questions with direct answers.
- Pay particular attention to instruction words: make sure you know what the examiner is asking you to do, then do it.

4
Research and planning

Discover what you need to know

One of the useful consequences of being set a specific essay title or question to complete is that it focuses your reading. If you approach a topic without a formulated question, then everything you read about that topic is - at least potentially - relevant to your interest. In contrast, when you have a clear mission you will zoom in on the parts of your reading that are most relevant, and skim those that don't relate directly to your topic of research. You become selective and driven. More creatively, when you are reading about an apparently unrelated topic, if you have the question you are supposed to be writing an answer to playing in the background of your mind, you will very likely, without effort, see parallels and contrasts that help you to understand the topic of your essay better.

Use reading lists

You will probably have been given a reading list. This will recommend more pages of writing than you could possibly read thoroughly in the time allocated. You need to be selective from within the reading. If a whole book is included, there is a good chance that large sections of it won't be relevant to the topic you are working on. So, be ruthless and put all your energy into the topics that *are* going to help you with your writing. Try to get an overview of a book before you get immersed in the details. Look carefully at the chapter headings for the information they contain. Skim the index to see where your main topic is most discussed in the book. Often the conclusion of a piece of writing gives extremely useful information about the general angle of the piece and the main arguments used. The key skill is getting straight to the relevant information or discussion. Don't feel obliged to begin on page one and plod through an entire book or article. That is going to waste far too much time. Don't feel guilty if you don't read a book from cover to cover. Remember that you will be judged by what you write, not by what you have read, and that essays are designed to test your ability to select relevant information and present it in a lively and well-structured way.

If you don't fully understand some of the terms used, consult a specialist dictionary, such as a dictionary of literary terms, a dictionary of psychology or a dictionary of philosophy. Some textbooks also include glossaries, which can be useful. Ordinary dictionaries are likely to be of only limited use. Don't be shy about consulting introductory books: often they give a far clearer picture of the essence of a topic and its key concepts than do the more advanced, and occasionally jargon-laden, works that will most likely appear on your reading list.

Stop researching and write something

An important skill is being able to stop the research process and begin writing. Many students go deeper and deeper into their topic before they begin to make an essay plan. They feel the need to do all the reading they possibly can before committing themselves to a structure. This is usually a mistake. Obviously, before you can plan out the detail of your answer you will need to have a good idea of the key issues you want to discuss. But that is not an adequate excuse for putting off the planning and even the first draft until you have very little time left in which to complete your assignment. Often it is only when you begin to plan your essay that you discover what you really need to know in order to give a good answer to the question. That might then take you back to your books and notes with a renewed enthusiasm and a specific piece of information to find.

Think on paper

Some thinking is best done on paper. You leave traces, you can see what you just thought, and you can draw links with arrows, delete, underline, and so on, modifying what you originally thought. Yet some students insist on thinking through their essay plan in their heads in a rather vague way – a kind of unfocused daydreaming around the topic. For most of us, jotting down ideas, seeing connections, capturing those thoughts that would otherwise drift just beyond memory, is the best way to approach the planning stage. Remember that no one else needs to see your plan. You should feel free to note possible directions your essay might take, but not to stick rigidly to these first thoughts if later they are out of place in the final structure.

You should try to establish your essay's structure as soon as possible. This involves working out what your angle on the question is, what your conclusion is going to be, what your main arguments are, and any counterarguments you are considering. You should be able to answer the following questions before beginning to write:

1   What is your main conclusion?
2   What arguments or evidence are you going to use to arrive at this conclusion?
3   Are there any counterarguments you need to consider?

You should also be asking yourself, even at the planning stage, 'Am I really answering the question set?' Your conclusion should be a direct response to that question. Having this written out on paper before you begin writing the essay is extremely useful.

Use the Internet

The Internet is a convenient source of huge amounts of unfiltered information and misinformation, some of it parasitic on unreliable evidence that gets recycled and paraphrased for each website. Much of what is available there would never have been published in a book – or at least not one published by a reputable publisher. Consequently, much of the information students download from the Internet is unreliable, and some is completely misleading. But even where the information *is* reliable, you should resist the temptation to cut and paste chunks of other people's writing into your essay. One reason is that this may amount to plagiarism (see Chapter 7). Just as importantly, students who use the Internet in this way often fail to analyse the material they quote in such large segments. Anyone can do an Internet search and then copy large amounts of information into an essay. The skill is in being selective and building up an argument to a conclusion using only material that is relevant to the question asked. Unless you develop your critical skills through thinking in writing about your subject, you won't develop as an essay writer, and you won't be awarded high marks.

It is also easy to get sidetracked into surfing the Internet as a possible source of ideas and waste many hours in the process. It is, however, particularly good for finding missing references (online library catalogues from reputable libraries, such as the British Library, the Cambridge University Library and the Oxford University

Bodleian Library, are very useful for this). The Internet is also good for finding facts, such as someone's date of birth or death, and his or her publications. You can also find reproductions of images, and these can be helpful for art historians, particularly when checking a detail of something you have seen elsewhere.

When using the Internet as a source, it is important only to get information from reliable sites. University websites are one starting point, as is the BBC. Be sceptical, though, about any information you find, and, if possible, double-check it.

Key points

- Having a formulated question will focus your research.
- Concentrate only on what is strictly relevant to your essay.
- Write a plan.
- Start writing sooner rather than later.
- Establish your conclusion and plan around that.
- Know the kinds of evidence you are going to use to support your conclusion.
- Don't waste time surfing the Internet; use it wisely and avoid cutting and pasting.

5
Beginnings, middles, ends

Beginnings

The blank sheet of paper, or, more often, the blank screen can be intimidating. You've planned your essay. You're ready. What next? How can you begin? Many student writers open their essays with rather vague speculation around the subject; some never get their essay on the right track again. The best opening lines, in contrast, are crisp and to the point. They often summarise the writer's conclusion or angle on the question asked and drive the essay forward from that point. The rest of the essay then builds a case to that conclusion.

Don't be tempted to fall back on dictionary definitions of key terms as a way of getting your essay launched. This is a clichéd way to open an essay, and almost always a mistake. It *is* a good idea to define or clarify keywords early on in the essay, to make clear what you are discussing. Copying out a dictionary definition, however, is often an avoidance of the more difficult and more interesting task of defining the word or phrase as it is used in the context implied by the question. Dictionaries are not likely to be particularly helpful with this sort of issue. If you can't resist the temptation to begin with a dictionary definition, try this strategy. Write your introductory sentence based on the definition; then delete it. Was anything important lost? Probably not. If not, don't reinstate it.

Most markers form an opinion of the essay writer's ability very early on. First impressions are extremely important. One of the best ways of creating a good first impression is to show that you are engaging immediately and critically with the specific question asked. Use some of the words of the question and engage with it head-on, steering the reader towards your argument and the case you make for your conclusion. If you are really struggling with those opening lines, then postpone writing them: pick a paragraph later on in your essay that you know you *can* write, and write that.

One of the delights of writing on a word processor is that you aren't obliged to write in the order you will be read. You can begin at the end of an essay, then write the introduction, then write the middle. When writing by hand, or using a typewriter, unless you are prepared to rewrite material it is very difficult to do this.

Middles

The middle of your essay is the filling in your sandwich. This is where your main argument takes place. Here each paragraph should do two things:

1   make a relevant point;
2   back it up with some kind of evidence, quotation, argument or example.

It really is that simple. There is no mystery about what each paragraph should do, but teachers rarely point this out to students. If you write a paragraph that fails to do either of these, then it probably won't make an important contribution to your essay. Obviously, the point that you make should be relevant to the question asked and should contribute to the case you are making for your conclusion. So, a third important feature of at least some of your paragraphs should be:

3   a sentence showing the relevance of what you have just said to the question asked.

Every paragraph that makes a relevant point and provides some evidence, quotation, argument or example to back it up contributes to your essay and moves it towards the goal of a well-supported conclusion.

Ends

The ending of your essay pulls the threads together and makes sure that your readers get the point of everything else included in the essay. Good concluding paragraphs can be very brief, sometimes even just a few sentences. A conclusion that replays the whole argument just set out is of no use to anyone. Trees shouldn't die to have you write the same thing twice (or in some cases three times). A concluding paragraph should refer back to the question, preferably picking up on the keywords of the question, and state very clearly your angle towards it. Avoid the temptation to end with a pithy statement or rhetorical question. Rhetorical questions are questions that are made for effect rather than to be answered. They are easy to write, but if you ask them you should answer them. Ending an essay with a rhetorical question will undermine your essay. Worse still is a string of rhetorical questions. The examiner or marker expects you to answer questions, not set new ones and leave them hanging.

Never end an academic essay with an exclamation mark, the crude punctuational equivalent of a nudge in the ribs: that's like saying 'Geddit?' at the end of a joke. Remember that the last impression you leave is the freshest in the reader's mind. For that reason, too, you should stop when you reach the end: don't keep tacking on further thoughts, otherwise you risk diluting the impact of your conclusion.

Key points

- First impressions are important: make sure your opening sentences are crisp and address the question.

43

- In the middle of your essay, each paragraph should make a point and back it up with some kind of evidence.
- Your conclusion needn't be long, but it should draw the threads of your argument together.

6
Making a case

Defend your conclusion

Think of your essay as an exercise in defending a conclusion and how you arrived at it. You should always have an angle on the question asked (i.e. you should know what you think about the main topic, or at least know the particular stance you are going to take on the issue for the sake of writing the essay). You will defend your conclusion by considering arguments and evidence for it, and, to a certain extent, against it too. By considering counterarguments and evidence against your own position, and demonstrating why these do not undermine your reasoning to your conclusion, you demonstrate the strength of your own arguments.

By the end of the essay the reader should be completely clear about where you stand on the question asked. If you're not clear about this, your reader certainly won't be. Your writing should be persuasive: that is, an intelligent person reading your essay should see the logic of your argument, the power of the evidence you provide in support of it, and so the rightness of your conclusion. Even if they disagree with you, they should be able to understand how you arrived at your conclusion and why you believe the weight of evidence lies in its favour.

Paragraphs as units of thought

The chief thing to remember is that, although paragraphing loses all point if the paragraphs are excessively long, the paragraph is essentially a unit of thought, not of length.

(Ernest Gowers, 1987, p. 170)

Paragraphs reveal the structure of your essay. They are the building blocks of your thought. There is no single right way to use paragraphs, but there are many confusing and irritating ways to use them. Starting a new paragraph every sentence is one of the more annoying twitches that some student essay-writers have – a style of writing perhaps derived from some tabloid journalism. It makes paragraphing redundant, as the full stop is doing exactly the same work as the paragraphing. It also has a stop–start feel to it, preventing the flow of ideas and making life hard for your reader.

Extremely long paragraphs are no use to anyone either, as the quotation from Ernest Gowers above makes clear. Well used, paragraphs can show when the author is addressing a new idea. If, however, your essay is just one long paragraph, or perhaps two or three (a beginning, a middle and an end), then very little is communicated by paragraphing. That is a very important opportunity missed.

Use signposts

The best essays use signposts to help the reader understand their structure. Signposts are sentences that give a clear indication of what the main topics covered in the paragraph are likely to be. For example, in an essay about the causes of the First World War, a student might write 'There were three main causes of the war' or 'The main cause of the war was . . .' or 'The second main cause of the war was . . .' or 'Several historians have argued against this conclusion. For instance, . . .' or 'To conclude . . .' These sentences and phrases prepare the reader for what is to come in the rest of the paragraph.

Ideally, you should begin every paragraph with some kind of summary of the main point of that paragraph, or at least a sentence that identifies what its main topic is. If you do this well, you should be able to take the first line of each paragraph and reconstruct the structure of the whole essay from this alone. Try it on an essay you wrote some time ago. Is it possible to add a few extra signpost sentences to help the reader see how the different parts of the essay fit together? If you have written a draft of an essay, go back over it and check that the first sentence of each paragraph is informative and provides directions to the reader about the function and content of that paragraph. Don't assume that the reader can simply follow the logic of your argument: make that logic visible with signposts.

Keep to the point

Don't digress. One key skill tested in essay writing, particularly in exams, is the ability to keep to the point. Every word you use in an interesting but irrelevant aside is a word wasted: you should want every word to count. The person reading your essay should never be able to think 'Yes, but so what?' The relevance of everything included should either be obvious or else be stated clearly. Keeping to the point is an aspect of answering the question set (rather than a different one), and so is crucial if you want to avoid the worst mistake of essay writing: *failing to answer the question*. At the very least, irrelevant material dilutes the power of your argument. It gives the marker the impression that you are not concentrating your efforts on the question set, but perhaps padding out your answer with some of the things that you have learnt and which you feel you want to get into the essay whatever question is set.

Consider counterarguments/ counterexamples

When you are making a case, a good way of developing your argument is by considering what can be said against it, and then responding to this imagined criticism. This involves playing different roles within the essay: sometimes putting your own arguments forward, sometimes addressing those arguments from the perspective of a critic. When you engage in this dialogue with yourself it is very important that you give clear signposts about which role you are taking at any particular point. So, for example, if you are defending the idea that the religious arguments against abortion outweigh any liberal arguments about women's rights to choose what happens in and to their bodies, then you will probably want to consider those liberal arguments in a strong form. When you introduce these counterarguments, you should use a signpost phrase such as 'Despite the powerful arguments about the sanctity of life, liberal philosophers such as Judith Jarvis Thomson have put a strong case for the view that a woman's right over her body should be paramount . . .' Then, if you have a reply to the liberal arguments, you need another signpost, such as 'A strong criticism of the liberal arguments above is . . .'

Argue to a conclusion

You've got to be careful if you don't know where you're going 'cause you might not get there.

(Yogi Berra, 1998)

The most important feature of a case well made is the conclusion, which should follow logically from what has gone before. Avoid the temptation to leave the readers to judge for themselves what the best answer to the question is: show them the way to your conclusion, and then provide it, leaving them in no doubt where you stand and why. The body of your essay should support your overall conclusion. And when you have reached your conclusion, stop.

Key points

- Make a case for your conclusion.
- Use paragraphs to develop the structure of your argument.
- Signpost sentences help the reader understand your essay's logic.
- Everything in your essay should be relevant to the question set. Cut irrelevant material.
- Don't leave the reader in any doubt about your conclusion or about the evidence supporting it.

7
Plagiarism, quotation, reference

Avoid plagiarism

Plagiarism is passing off someone else's work as your own. Don't do it. It is a dangerous and immoral thing to do. And sometimes it is illegal. This is obvious. If I had copied out large sections of someone else's book and then published it as if it were my own words, then I would have done something that is both immoral and illegal. I would have stolen their work and passed it off as if I had written it myself. Copyright laws provide authors with a defence against this sort of theft, but these laws don't just apply to published authors: they apply to students too.

In the age of the Internet it is very easy for students to get access to other students' writing and to copy and paste it into their essays as if it were their own work. If you are rich enough and foolish enough, you can also buy other people's essays on the Internet. Many who do this then simply hand the essays in with their own name on them.

Copying from books without using quotation marks or references to indicate that words are not your own is the traditional form of plagiarism, and it is still quite common. Even if you do this by mistake, perhaps because of poor note-taking that doesn't distinguish your own thoughts from someone else's, you are very likely to be accused of plagiarism if found out. The severity of penalty for plagiarism varies, but in extreme cases students will be given a mark of zero and prevented from retaking exams. They may even be prosecuted.

Anyone who uses this approach to education lacks imagination. Apart from the moral and legal issues, plagiarism is foolish for several other reasons too. First, you are likely to get caught: software now exists that is very good at tracking down stolen words. And if you are caught, the consequences are likely to be very serious.

Second, even if you get away with it, you lose the opportunity of thinking things through for yourself. As I have already stressed, writing is a kind of thinking. If you don't write your own essays, you will never get many of the benefits of education. You may end up passing a course without really understanding anything. You might not regret this immediately, but looking back in later years you will very likely recognise a lost opportunity and a bad decision. If you get into a college or get a job on the basis of this sort of cheating, you may get found out at a later stage and your whole career could be undermined. You may end up feeling that you are a fraud, even if no one else ever knows what you have done.

The simplest way to avoid the charge of plagiarism is to be systematic about your use of references and to use quotation marks whenever you use someone else's words. This is important in your notes as well as in your essays: it is very easy when coming back to notes written months earlier to forget that the words weren't your own but someone else's. This is a common cause of accidental plagiarism and is far less blameworthy than deliberate deception. Try to establish good habits in this matter, always using quotation marks to indicate quotations even in very rough drafts of your essays.

Can you plagiarise your own work? Probably not. But you should acknowledge that you have already written the same words in a different context, particularly if there is likely to be a question of whether you have had the same piece of work count twice towards a grade. In that spirit, I'd like to acknowledge that I've already used the five examples below in a study skills book directed specifically at philosophy students, *Philosophy: The Essential Study Guide* (Warburton, 2004):

Plagiarism, paraphrase and exposition: five examples

1 If the sceptic is right, then each of us is in an important way detached from the world around us. You know nothing about the world out there. You have no reason at all to believe that you inhabit a world of trees, houses, cats, dogs, mountains and cars. And you have no reason at all to think that you are surrounded by other people. For all you know, your entire world – including all the people in it – is merely virtual.

Comment: This is a direct yet unacknowledged quotation from p. 53 of Stephen Law's excellent introduction to philosophy, *The Philosophy Files* (London: Orion, 2000). The only difference between what is written above and what is in the book is that I have removed two comments which are in brackets in the original. If I had written this as a paragraph in a philosophy essay without quotation marks or acknowledgement of its source, it would be a clear case of plagiarism. It would still be counted as plagiarism even if I had simply forgotten to put in the quotation marks; though I might not be so culpable, it is unlikely that anyone marking this would give me the benefit of the doubt.

2 Imagine for the sake of argument that the sceptic is right. In that case each of us is in an important way detached from the external world. We know nothing of the world out there. We have no reason at all to believe that there are trees, houses, cats, mountains, etc. For all you know, your whole world, including everyone in it, is a virtual one.

Comment: Again this is plagiarism, though not in such a blatant form as in the first passage. Although I have paraphrased the original, the syntax, examples and sentence structure are so similar to the original that the derivation is still obvious. Furthermore, there is no acknowledgement whatsoever of the original source. The only plausible justification for such paraphrase would be to avoid the charge that it is simply an unacknowledged quotation; there is no philosophical justification for simply rewriting a passage in slightly different words.

> 3 Stephen Law says that if the sceptic is right, 'then each of us is in an important way detached from the world around us'. Then we have no reason to believe that we inhabit a world of 'trees, houses, cats, dogs, mountains and cars'. And we have no reason to believe in the existence of other people. For all you know, 'your entire world – including all the people in it' is merely virtual.

Comment: This time, although the writer acknowledges the source of the quotation, this passage is simply a collage of quotations – some marked by quotation marks, others not. Although this might escape the charge of plagiarism, it is still a very weak way of summarising a passage and demonstrates no understanding of the passage summarised. The main ideas are simply parroted. Most essays will involve a certain amount of summary and exposition of others' ideas. The art of summary, however, is not an art of cut and paste. It involves explanation and, preferably, the use of some fresh examples rather than the reuse of just those in the original text.

> 4 In *The Philosophy Files*, Stephen Law summarises the sceptical position: 'each of us is in an important way detached from the world around us. You know nothing about the world out there' (p. 53). Most importantly, he emphasises that a sceptic has no reason for believing in the existence of other people. Our experiences, which seem to be of other people, may be misleading. We may in fact be looking at holograms, or else be plugged into a virtual reality machine which creates the illusion of our seeing, hearing, touching, feeling and smelling other people.

Comment: This passage both summarises and explains the ideas in Law's paragraph. It also acknowledges the source of the quotation, and puts the idea that we may be plugged into a virtual reality machine in the essay writer's own words. This is a case not of plagiarism, but of the sort of exposition that would be appropriate in a philosophy essay.

> 5 Most of us, most of the time are convinced that the world we perceive with our senses exists and is more or less as it appears to us. Sceptics challenge our complacency about this. They argue that we have no more reason to believe that such things as walls, tables, chairs, feet and goldfish actually exist than that they don't. All these things may be imaginary. Furthermore, other people may not exist. Sceptics entertain the idea that what we take to be experience may be created by someone manipulating us: we may simply be plugged into a highly sophisticated virtual reality machine, even if we don't realise this is the case. The key point is that for the sceptic there is no more reason to believe that things are as they seem than that they aren't.

Comment: This passsage addresses the same ideas as the quotation from Stephen Law, but it does so in a way that makes clear that I have understood the ideas being expressed and have made them my own to such a degree that there is probably no need to indicate in the main text that they were inspired by the passage in Law's book (though it would be appropriate in such circumstances to include a reference to Law's book in the bibliography). If in doubt, though, it is always safer to include mention of the original source, and you are unlikely ever to be penalised for this.*

* For this reason, I should mention that the idea for laying out examples of plagiarism in this way came from a handout written in 1989 by Richard Dennis of the University College London Geography department, though I have used my own examples and have included more explanation of them than he does.

Use quotation marks

Whenever you quote someone else you need to communicate this fact to your reader. The simplest way is to put the other person's words within single inverted commas. So you might write:

> Nigel Warburton, in his book *The Basics of Essay Writing* (2006), wrote that 'essay writing is at the heart of education'.

If you omit quotation marks in cases like this, you may be branded a plagiarist. Here I have used an indentation to indicate that the whole sentence above is a quotation. This technique is usual for longer quotations. If, however, you find yourself using longer quotations, you should ask yourself whether they are really necessary. If your essay is broken up by numerous longer quotations, you are probably using cut and paste as an alternative to critical thought. An academic essay should be a critical argument to a conclusion, not a collage of quotations. To justify the inclusion of any longer quotation you must be sure to *analyse* that quotation rather than to treat its presence as self-explanatory.

Give clear references and a bibliography

References are the notes indicating the precise source (page number, etc.) of quoted lines, or paraphrased ideas. A bibliography is a list, in alphabetical order (by author surname), of all the works consulted or referred to when writing your essay, including books, articles and web pages. Bibliographies usually appear at the very end of an essay. Consistency of style in writing references or a bibliography is very important: without this consistency, confusions can arise. Most tutors give guidance on the reference system you are to use. If your tutor leaves the choice to you, read this section and select the system for giving references that seems most straightforward.

The main reasons for giving references and a bibliography are 1) so that other people can locate the sources of your ideas if they want to; and 2) to avoid the charge of plagiarism.

There are several different acceptable conventions on giving references. The main information you need to communicate in your bibliography is the author's name, the title of the book, and usually the place, publisher and the date of its publication. If the entry is for an article, the journal title and volume/issue number, together with the page references for the article, are key.

The two main ways of indicating sources are 1) including most of the information in a footnote or endnote (an endnote is a note at the end of the essay); and 2) including basic information in brackets in the main text of your essay, and full bibliographical information in the bibliography at the end of your essay. This second style of referencing is sometimes known as the 'author/date' system. If you are using this system and either referring to or quoting from a specific page or pages, then you should include the page number as well as the author and date. It is easier to see the difference between these two styles by looking at examples:

In his novel *The Spire* (1), William Golding portrays a man driven by sexual passion who interprets this as divine calling.

1. Golding, William, *The Spire*, London: Faber, 1954

In his novel *The Spire* (Golding, 1954) William Golding portrays a man driven by sexual passion who interprets this as divine calling.

Bibliography

Golding, William (1954) *The Spire*, London: Faber.

A very widely used convention that you should be aware of is to underline or italicise book titles and to put article or chapter titles within inverted commas. So, *Philosophy: The Basics* or <u>Philosophy: The Basics</u> would clearly be a book; whereas 'Freedom to Box', because it is within inverted commas, is either an article or a chapter heading. Once you have realised this, you will glean more information from scanning through a bibliography than you would have done previously. It is surprising how few students are aware of this convention. Another convention is to put URLs of Internet sites within this sort of bracket: <>, and to give the date when you consulted the site (since sites may be updated). If you don't put the Internet site within brackets of some kind, your reader may be confused about whether a full stop or other item of punctuation is part of the address or not.

Key points

- Don't plagiarise.
- Always acknowledge your sources by using quotation marks and, if appropriate, a bibliography.
- Keep references consistent.

8
The craft of writing

Have something to say and say it as clearly as you can. That is the only secret of style.

(Matthew Arnold)

Get the tone right

One of the surest ways of irritating your reader is to use colloquial language or a conversational style in an academic essay. The tone or register of what you write can be as important as its content. The academic essay is the wrong place to experiment with writing styles; save the experimentation for a creative writing class or your private notebooks, letters, emails or text messages. It is difficult to lay down guidelines about what is acceptable in this respect, but it is important to develop an ear for the appropriate language to use.

Here is an extreme case. If a student writes an essay using the spelling conventions of a text message – '2day' for 'today' or 'evng' for 'evening', for example – this creates a bad impression no matter how brilliant the essay's content. It shows insensitivity to the academic context. While text message abbreviations are effective in text messages, and some journalistic writing and advertising copywriting too, they are completely inappropriate in a student essay (unless, perhaps that essay is about different spelling conventions, in which case they would appear within inverted commas as *examples of* rather than *uses of* the words). Here are some more examples of inappropriate colloquialisms:

- 'Loads of writers admire Shakespeare's imagery' [use 'many']
- 'In *The Merchant of Venice*, Antonio and his mates tease Shylock' [use 'his friends']

- 'My favourite poem is Shelley's 'Ozymandias' – it is <u>wicked</u>' [use 'a remarkable poem' or equivalent]
- 'Othello <u>loses his rag</u> when he thinks Desdemona has betrayed him' [use 'loses his temper']

Five symptoms of an inappropriate tone

- Use of *exclamation marks* (unless within quotations). Worse still are double exclamation marks, e.g. 'King Duncan doesn't realise that the Macbeths are planning to murder him!!'
- Use of *slang* (again, unless within quotations), e.g. 'Banquo is a diamond geezer.'
- *Chattiness*: e.g. 'Well that's enough of my random thoughts, let's have a look at what the author says on the topic.'
- *One-sentence paragraphs.* These are only really acceptable in tabloid journalism. On rare occasions they may be acceptable, but consecutive single-sentence paragraphs are almost always a mark of inappropriate tone.
- *Jokey comments*: e.g. 'Shakespeare's Macbeth (now there's a hen-pecked guy!) hallucinates a dagger . . . What was he on?'

One way of developing sensitivity to academic writing and markers' expectations is to look at other students' essays, preferably alongside the feedback received from markers. This is a good way of understanding the range of styles of writing that a question can elicit. Another strategy is to try reading your own work aloud; this is an excellent technique for achieving a distance from your own writing, a distance that can allow you to develop a critical stance towards some aspects of it.

Be economical with adjectives

Adjectives are words that colour prose: they describe nouns. 'The *quick sly* fox with *reddish* hair dashes through the *glistening wet* undergrowth' contains five adjectives (all italicised). The best writers use adjectives with care. Try to avoid using more than one adjective to describe a single item: so write 'Hardy's bleak prose' rather than 'Hardy's bleak, sombre and dark prose'. If you use strings of adjectives, your essays will read like the worst kind of creative writing.

Punctuate effectively

Apostrophes

Apostrophes are very small, and misusing them is a minor mistake. Nevertheless, you should be aware that some examiners get very irritated by students who don't know how to use them. Their irritation is often out of all proportion to the seriousness of the mistake: when students misuse apostrophes there is rarely any ambiguity about what they mean. Despite this, though, many people can't help getting twitchy when they notice missing or, worse still, inappropriate apostrophes. You may think 'Well, that's their problem', but irritating your examiner could affect your overall grade. You may not lose marks directly for that missing bit of punctuation, but you may have suggested to the examiner that you are not quite a first-rate student. This is not a good policy. If you ever make mistakes with apostrophes it is worth taking twenty minutes to break this habit.

There are two uses of the apostrophe: to indicate a letter or letters that have been left out; and to indicate possession.

Missing letters

- 'It's' is short for 'it is', as in 'It's easy to improve.' (Don't confuse this with 'its', which means 'belonging to it' as in 'the dog bit its own tail'.)
- 'Don't' is short for 'do not'.
- 'Can't' is short for 'cannot'.
- 'Who's' is short for 'who is', as in 'Who's afraid of Virginia Woolf?' (Don't confuse this with 'whose', which is the possessive of 'who', as in 'the man whose car is parked outside'.)

Possession

The simplest cases are when the word doesn't end in an 's', e.g. 'The dog's dinner', 'the cat's whiskers'. When you are talking about more than one dog or cat, these should be 'the dogs' dinner' and 'the cats' whiskers'.

Note that when a plural doesn't end in 's', such as 'children', you simply add the apostrophe and then an 's': so you would write 'the children's playground'.

When you have a name that ends in 's', there are two different conventions. You should choose one or the other and be consistent:

1 Convention 1: just add the apostrophe as in 'Paris' suburbs' or 'Caruthers' book'.
2 Convention 2: add the apostrophe followed by a further 's', as in 'Paris's suburbs' or 'Caruthers's book'.

The commonest mistakes that students make are leaving the apostrophe out altogether, writing phrases such as 'Hardys novel' rather than 'Hardy's novel'. More irritating still is putting in extra apostrophes: some students add them when they use a plural, e.g. 'Second World War pilot's won the Battle of Britain'. Here there is neither a missing letter nor any possession, so the apostrophe shouldn't be used.

If you are unsure about apostrophes, get a friend to copy out a short passage from something you are reading, leaving out all the apostrophes. Try putting them in yourself and see how you get on.

Commas

A common mistake is to leave out the second of two parenthetical commas. 'Parenthesis' is another word for bracketing off something. With this use of commas, omitting the second comma is like failing to put in a second bracket. So, for example, in the sentence I'm writing, the words 'for example' are bracketed off between two commas. Had I only included the first example thus: 'So, for example in the sentence I'm writing . . .' then the function of the first comma would be confusing. Look for missing second commas of this kind when you are revising your work.

Colons and semicolons

What colons are good for: fulfilling the promise expressed in the first part of a sentence (as in this sentence). Semicolons are useful when you want to break up a list that includes several quite long items; they are also effective when you want to balance two parts of a sentence (as in the one you are reading now). However, if you don't feel confident using long sentences split by semicolons, it is much safer to use a full stop, breaking a longer sentence in two. In the case of my own sentence above I could quite easily have written: 'Semicolons are useful when you want to break up a list that includes several quite long items. They are also effective when you want to balance two parts of a sentence.' I suspect that the two-sentence version is slightly easier to follow. If you agree, then think hard before you write a long sentence. It might be better to split it into two or more shorter sentences, either as you write, or at the editing stage.

Exclamation marks

Don't use exclamation marks unless you are quoting something that includes them. You can probably get away with one exclamation mark or perhaps two in an essay, but why take the risk? Exclamation marks are like heavy nudges in the ribs: not really appropriate for the tone of an academic essay. Resist the temptation to use this form of punctuation. It is unlikely that any academic essay has ever been improved by using exclamation marks.

Use the active voice

One of the easiest ways to make your writing more direct is to eliminate passive constructions. Use only active constructions. 'The Romans defeated the Britons' is an active use of the verb 'defeated'. 'The Britons were defeated by the Romans' is a passive use. Notice that the first sentence has only five words, whereas the second has seven. But apart from the passive being a more wordy way of expressing the same idea, it is more difficult to unravel when reading. Clear, straightforward sentences are expressed in the active. Good writers rarely use the passive voice.

Officials in government often use passive constructions, perhaps at times to make what they are saying slightly opaque. As Harold Evans, the newspaper editor, commented, Churchill's direct declaration 'Give us the tools and we will finish the job' easily trumps its translation into the style of an official communication: 'The task would be capable of determination were the appropriate tools to be made available to those concerned' (Harold Evans, *Essential English*, p. 24).

Here are some examples of passive constructions that use an impersonal 'it'. Avoid them:

- It is often argued that
- It is the case that/It is not the case that
- It is believed that
- It cannot be denied that
- It will be recognised that
- It should be pointed out that
- It was felt necessary
- It should be noted that

Impersonal passives conceal who is arguing, believing, denying and so on; they also add unnecessary words to your essay. When you read through a draft, look out for these phrases and wherever possible rewrite sentences that contain them.

A note about conventions in science

The standard convention for writing scientific reports and papers is to write them in the passive voice. So, for example, your teacher may expect you to write up a chemistry experiment impersonally: rather than 'I heated the liquid in the test tube until it boiled', your description might read 'the liquid in the test tube was heated until it boiled'. Teachers may also ask you to write up experiments or surveys in the social sciences using this convention. Be sure that you know whether this is the convention that your teacher or lecturer wants you to use. If it isn't, then eliminate passive constructions altogether.

Avoid convoluted sentences

The easiest way to avoid convoluted sentences is to write short to medium-length ones. Avoid long sentences altogether in exams. If you find a sentence winding on from one line to the next and to the next, then it is probably too long. There is a straightforward solution. Find a place to break the sentence, then rewrite it as two shorter sentences (see below for an example). A succession of very short, abrupt sentences can be almost as difficult to read as a long one. The most stylish essay writers as a matter of second nature avoid writing long and syntactically complex sentences. Nevertheless, some academics do welcome longer sentences, but only well-structured ones, as the following quotation from Thomas Dixon's book *How to Get a First* makes clear. Notice that he actually illustrates his points by using longer and shorter sentences as he is writing about them:

> Academics disagree amongst themselves about sentences. Some favour short ones. Others are quite happy, indeed enthusiastic, about the idea that students should, in the course of their studies, cultivate the art of the long sentence; being able to retain control of one's ideas and language while constructing a complex and involved sentence, making judicious use of commas and semi-colons, they say, is an important academic skill. I prefer brevity. There is no need to adopt a hard and fast rule about this though. Sometimes a long and involved sentence might be appropriate and attractive. In my experience of reading and marking student essays, however, their sentences seem to be too long more often than they are too short.
>
> (Dixon, 2004, pp. 148–9)

If you must write longer sentences, make sure they aren't convoluted. Don't make the reader work too hard to extract meaning from what you have written. The safest policy is always to write short to medium-length sentences. This is an aspect of the best general advice for writers: 'be concise'.

Be concise

In their classic short book on writing, *The Elements of Style* (2000), Strunk and White's most important piece of advice is contained in three words that make up a section heading, 'Omit needless words'. This is explained in slightly more detail:

> Vigorous writing is concise. A sentence should contain no unnecessary words, a paragraph no unnecessary sentences, for the same reason that a drawing should have no unnecessary lines and a machine no unnecessary parts. This requires not that the writer make all sentences short, or avoid all detail and treat subjects only in outline, but that every word tell.
>
> (Strunk and White, 2000, p. 23)

This is excellent advice. Follow it. Notice too that by following their own advice Strunk and White could probably have reduced this instruction to two words: be concise.

Avoid adverbs

Adverbs are words which describe the verb in a sentence. So, for example, I have underlined the adjectives in the short passage below. They usually end in 'ly'.

> The fish swim <u>quickly</u> upstream, afraid that the dark waters might <u>totally</u> engulf them. <u>Swiftly</u> they flash past the river bank, <u>steadfastly</u> driving onwards to their breeding grounds.

Adverbs have their uses, but their frequent use almost always detracts from the directness of writing. Even if you are a creative writer, pay careful attention to their use. If you are editing your work, try going on an adverb hunt. For each adverb tracked down in your writing, decide whether anything has been lost by removing it. If something is lost, is there a better way of expressing the same idea?

Avoid clichés

A cliché is an overused phrase. The word 'cliché' is pejorative: calling something a cliché suggests that it is a bad use of English. So the judgement that a phrase is a cliché is already a judgement that it is something to avoid. Here are some examples:

at the end of the day
barking up the wrong tree
a can of worms
the dim and distant past
can't see the wood for the trees
dire straits
far and away
glutton for punishment
great minds think alike
in this day and age
in the nick of time
new lease of life
silent majority
the fact of the matter is . . .
throw the baby out with the bathwater
tower of strength
well and truly
with the best will in the world

You should avoid clichés wherever possible as they make your writing dull: think how little would have been added to this last sentence if I'd written 'as dull as ditchwater' in place of 'dull'. Your ideas won't seem fresh if they are presented using these familiar expressions. Clichés also contribute to a journalistic or colloquial tone that is inappropriate for academic writing. Most of us use clichés in speech and in writing without recognising it, or at least without worrying about it. Becoming aware of clichés in your writing can be an important step towards clearer and more precise self-expression.

Learn from others' clarity

If you come across a piece of writing that seems particularly clear, try to work out how the writer has achieved this effect. Perhaps even copy out the passage, adding your own notes below it. If you get the opportunity to read other students' essays on a topic on which you have written, take it. Ask yourself whether the writer is easy or difficult to follow. Most students have very little idea about how people reading their work will experience it.

Avoid these common mistakes

alternate/alternative: When used as an adjective, 'alternate' means one then the other, as in the instruction to use alternate legs for an aerobics exercise; an 'alternative' is a choice.

complement/compliment: These are two different words. If something complements something else, it makes it complete. This is an easy way of remembering which (complement/compliment) is which; look at the spelling of 'complement' and 'complete'. A compliment, in contrast, is praise.

criterion/criteria: 'Criterion' is the singular, 'criteria' the plural. So don't write 'a criteria'.

disinterested/uninterested: A common mistake is to think that 'disinterested' means 'bored by'. It doesn't. Disinterested research is unbiased research. Don't write 'He was disinterested' when you mean 'he was uninterested' (i.e. bored by).

e.g./i.e.: 'E.g.' means 'for example, as in 'there are many carnivorous animals, e.g. lions and tigers'. What follows 'e.g.' is simply a specific instance of something more general. 'I.e.' means 'that is'. Whatever follows 'i.e.' must be the equivalent of what has just been stated, as in 'the writer who was known as George Orwell, i.e. Eric Blair'. Contrast this with 'There are many well-known writers who have used pseudonyms, e.g. the writers known as Lewis Carroll, George Eliot and George Orwell.'

fewer/less: Use 'fewer' when you are writing about individual things; 'less' when you are referring to quantity that doesn't divide up into units. This is easier to demonstrate than explain. 'There are fewer people here today than yesterday' is correct. 'There are less people here' is incorrect. 'There is less water in the tank' is correct. 'I have less money in my pocket' is correct, as is 'I have fewer coins in my pocket', but 'I have less coins' is incorrect.

its/it's: 'It's' is short for 'it is', as in 'It's Tuesday.' 'Its' is the possessive of 'it', as in 'The dog wagged its tail.' If you have a tendency to muddle these two, make sure you check through your work at the editing stage.

literally: Sentences such as 'he was literally over the moon', unless used to describe astronauts, show that the writer doesn't understand the meaning of the word 'literally' (in this case too, unless used ironically, the cliché 'over the moon' should be avoided). When you edit your work, the safest and most stylish option is to cut out all uses of 'literally'. If you do want to use the word, make sure you avoid absurdity.

phenomenon/phenomena: 'Phenomenon' is the singular, 'phenomena' the plural. So don't write 'a phenomena'.

principle/principal: a principle is a rule or guideline; 'principal' means 'main', or in the United States it is the head teacher in a school (hence the American mnemonic 'your principal is your pal').

refute/repudiate: If you refute a statement, you demonstrate that it is false. If you repudiate it, you simply deny it.

stationery/stationary: Stationery is paper, envelopes, etc. 'Stationary' means not moving.

their/there/they're: 'Their' is a possessive, as in 'They put on their hats'; 'there' is a place, as in 'over there'; 'they're' is an abbreviation of 'they are'. Most people know the difference between these three words, but even some university students confuse 'there' and 'their', so it is worth checking your work through before handing it in to make sure that you have used the correct form of these homonyms (words that sound the same). Getting them wrong is likely to colour the marker's impression of you.

77

Avoid sexist language

Some ways of phrasing your essay can appear sexist. For example, if you talk about 'man' or 'mankind' when you mean to include women as well, you run the risk of coming across as sexist even if that is not your general stance on the world. If, for example, you describe archaeology as 'the study of man's past through his arte-facts', you seem to be excluding women and their artefacts from the study. There are various ways in which you can avoid this charge of sexism. One is to use 'humanity' rather than 'man'. Here are some terms which may come across as sexist, together with a more neutral alternative for each:

actress – actor
air hostess – flight attendant
chairman – chair
fireman – firefighter
foreman – supervisor
layman – layperson
mankind – humankind
masterpiece – work of genius, iconic work
policeman – police officer
salesman – salesperson (though, obviously, you shouldn't alter the
    title of Arthur Miller's play *Death of a Salesman*)
weatherman – weather forecaster
workman – worker

Don't use 'he' (or 'she') when you mean 'he or she'. One option is to use 'they', as in 'If a headteacher is involved they should fill in a record of the meeting' rather than 'If a headteacher is involved he should fill in a record of the meeting.' The second of these two examples gives the impression that all headteachers are male. The first, however, is rather awkward. A far better solution in many cases is to rephrase the sentence so that you are using a plural noun. In the case above, this would give us 'If headteachers are involved they should fill in a record of the meeting.' As you can see from this example, however, this may change nuances of meaning. You need to be sensitive to individual cases and find an alternative that captures the meaning you want to express. Even if you don't happen to believe that the use of 'he' for 'he or she' is sexist, it probably isn't worth risking using 'he' in this context as the person marking your essay may feel quite differently about this.

Spelling

In the age of electronic spell-checkers it is very easy to conceal poor spelling. However, most students aren't allowed to use spell-checkers in exams. So, it is a good idea to put in a few hours to make sure that you don't make basic spelling mistakes, not because you are likely to have marks deducted for poor spelling, but rather because poor spelling may colour an examiner's view of you.

The most important spellings to get right are the names of people, characters, places, books, poems, paintings, etc. that are the subject matter of your essay. Make sure that you know how to spell these. It is very simple to make a list of the key proper names that occur in your subject. Some names, such as 'Nietzsche', are very difficult to spell: it is worth putting in some time learning these, as if you get them wrong you may give the examiner the impression that you don't care very much about the subject.

Apart from names, there are many words which students struggle to spell. Below is a list of words that students often misspell. Skim over it to see whether you know all the spellings: if not, create your own list of difficult words. Recognise that we all have difficulty with some words, but you can eliminate some obvious mistakes, and in the process give a much better impression to the person reading your essay.

Difficult spellings

abbreviation
absence
accident
accommodation
achieve
acknowledge
acquire
address
adjacent
advertisement
analogous
annihilate
antecedent
apparatus
apparently
appreciate
approach
argument
artefact
basically
beautiful
beginning
believe
buried
business
caricature
census

character
chronological
colleague
committee
conceit
conceive
condemn
consensus
courtesy
deceive
despair
despise
dilemma
ecstasy
efficient
embarrass, embarrassment
environment
exercise
exorcise (or exorcize)
existence
extraordinary
fulfil
glamour, glamorous
government
gruesome
hoi polloi
humorist

Spelling

humour, humorous
idiosyncrasy
idiosyncratic
illiterate
immigration
in flagrante
incendiary
incentive
incomprehensible
indigenous
independent
indispensable
inoculate
instil
irresponsible
itinerary
jeopardy
judgement
knowledgeable
literary
literature
medieval
millennium
necessary
non sequitur
noticeable
obscene
obsolete
occasion
occur
occurred
omit
parliament

playwright
possession
prerogative
properly
psychiatric
psychiatrist
psychological
questionnaire
really
receipt
receive
recommend
repeat
repetition
restaurant
rhyme
rhythm
schedule
seize
separate
siege
solemn
stationary
stupefy
subtle, subtlety
succeed
success, successful
summary
supersede
surreptitious
symbol
temperature
threshold

transfer, transferable, transferred,   Wednesday
  transferring   withhold
vicious   written
viscous   xenophobia

Key points

- The tone of your writing should be appropriate for an academic essay.
- Small mistakes, such as misplaced apostrophes, can have a disproportionate effect on a marker's impression of your work.
- Avoid passive constructions, adverbs and overuse of adjectives.
- Be concise.

9
The exam essay

Understand the genre

The examination essay is a genre in itself. Most examinations require you to write several essays in quite a short period of time. This severely limits what you can say, particularly if you are not allowed to bring notes or books into the examination room. There is almost no scope for rewriting: any corrections after the first draft are likely to be minimal. You may find that you scarcely have time to reread what you have written before handing it in. Consequently, if you want to succeed in this genre you will need to adjust your writing style accordingly. You will also need to be aware of what is possible within the time constraints: if you expect to achieve too much in the allotted time, you may set off at the wrong pace and never arrive at your conclusion.

The basic principles of essay writing I have outlined in the rest of this book apply to examination essays too, but the emphasis is somewhat different. The three most important principles of good examination essay technique are:

1   Answer the question set.
2   Make a case.
3   Omit unnecessary words.

Examination essays need to be focused and direct. There is no time to waste words, follow digressions or quote extensively. Nor will you have time to write a long plan. A typical examination essay in the humanities subjects will make three or four main points, perhaps one per paragraph of the essay, and these points will build to the conclusion expressed in the final paragraph (and perhaps also mentioned in the introduction). Realising how little you will be able to write within an examination should focus your preparation.

Be prepared

The best preparation for writing under examination essays is writing practice plans and practice essays under examination conditions. If you want to improve your examination performance, you will have to face up to this. Forty-five minutes spent planning and writing a practice essay will be far more effective for most students than several hours of rereading notes. As with all writing, you may find that you rationalise why you needn't write a practice essay. Perhaps you intend to do one tomorrow, not today. You might find all kinds of other distractions and avoidance strategies. But if you really want to perform better in examinations you do need to practise the activity that you will be judged on, or something very close to it. Most students only devote a tiny fraction of their revision time to practising essay plans and essay writing, but ultimately their final grades will depend on whether they can write essays under these challenging conditions.

Set yourself timed essays on topics you understand thoroughly. Don't be tempted to write a practice essay on a vague topic: set a specific question for yourself, either one that has come up in a past examination, or one that you think might well come up in the future. The exercise of inventing possible examination questions is itself very instructive: there are usually very few plausible questions that can be asked about any particular topic. You may even find that you second-guess the examiner and prepare a practice question that is very close to the one you end up writing in the examination. That isn't the main point of the exercise, however. The main reason for writing practice plans and essays is to get into the habit of writing to the appropriate length at the right pace, answering the question set, and of making a case for a conclusion rather than listing a series of unconnected facts.

Once you have a suitable question, write it out. Plan your answer; then write the essay itself. Next, the really painful bit:

read the essay back, preferably aloud. You should be able to hear how the essay is going, whether you have managed to achieve an appropriate style, whether your reasoning is plausible or not, and so on. You will very soon realise how much easier it is to read prose written in short or medium-length sentences rather than in long ones. As you read, ask yourself these three fundamental questions:

1   Have I *really* answered the question set?
2   Have I made a good case for the conclusion I've given?
3   Have I omitted unnecessary words?

If you have a friend taking the same course, you might ask that friend to listen as you reread the essay and to consider those three questions too.

Use active revision techniques

In general, active revision techniques are the best. Find ways of engaging critically with the material you need to learn; don't just read and reread your notes or set books. For instance, if you have half an hour to spend on revision, you might set yourself three exam questions and write ten-minute plans for each. In your essay plan, try to map out a defence of a conclusion using evidence and argument, following the principles stressed in this book. This should then take you back to your notes and books as you realise where the gaps in your knowledge are. Test yourself on what you know, or test a friend. Rewrite your notes into a shorter, more memorable form. Whatever revision techniques you use, try to make sure that you have a clear goal: don't waste time in unfocused reading. Passive revision takes less energy, but it won't get you where you want to be unless you are very lucky.

Coping with exam nerves

Most people find exams stressful. Who hasn't felt their heart race, their palms sweat, and even a sinking feeling in the pit of their stomach when standing outside an exam room waiting to go in? This stress, if channelled, can be a source of energy and focus. It is a sign that you are taking the exam seriously. Some people, however, find exams so stressful that they never realise their potential under exam conditions. They get into a cycle of increasing stress that blocks their ability to think clearly and in extreme cases prevents them from writing at all.

One of the best ways to minimise the effect of exam nerves and to stop them spiralling out of control is to be well prepared. That way you can be confident that you will be able to answer the questions set. If you have done some timed essay writing outside the exam room, you will be aware of how little you can write under these conditions and how important it is to focus your answer. In this way you reduce the risk of having the nasty surprise of finding that time has run out halfway through your final essay. At the very least you will have got used to writing by hand at speed. Good revision, then, should eliminate some of the causes of exam nerves. It won't eliminate all nerves, though, and that is probably as well. The flow of adrenaline can improve your performance as long as you don't let your anxiety get out of control.

In the days and then hours coming up to an exam it is extremely important to keep the whole matter in perspective. Getting adequate sleep is one way of helping to achieve this. Some people have managed to get excellent results on very few hours' sleep, but this isn't easy. It isn't just the night before the exam that matters; try to avoid building up a sleep deficit in the week or so before you take the exam. Avoid drinking coffee or tea in the evening and don't stay up until the early hours revising. This is likely to be counter-productive and get you into bad sleep patterns that are hard to break.

Coping with exam nerves

Remember that the quality of your revision is only one key to success; another is being alert in the exam itself. You need to realise that no matter how well your revision has gone, you will need to think during the exam, not simply regurgitate facts.

If your revision hasn't gone well, or your sleep has been disrupted, you may feel the temptation to catastrophise: to see the worst possible outcome as if it had already happened. In this case you might think that you won't be able to pass the exam. You can convince yourself that you have failed even before you've seen the question paper. But these negative thoughts can actually make it more likely that you won't succeed; far better to be positive, and to remember that even if your revision hasn't gone perfectly, you will have a reasonable chance of passing the exam if you have good exam technique and can organise what you do know well within your essays.

Rather than sit worrying about what terrible things might happen in the exam room, set some time aside to build up a positive and imaginative pre-visualisation of giving a superb performance in the exam. This is time well spent. See yourself relaxed yet alert going into the exam room to find your name on your desk. You turn over the exam paper and read through all the questions carefully. You mark the ones you want to attempt, and feel confident that you can give good, well-structured responses to each one. You have written down the finishing time for each essay. You plan and then write each essay in a calm and fluent way, and everything you have studied on the subject comes back to you effortlessly. Each of your essays makes a well-argued case for a conclusion that relates directly to the question asked. Whenever you make a general point you back it up with evidence or quotation. You finish five minutes before the allotted time and use the extra minutes to go over your paper, eliminating minor mistakes of punctuation, spelling, etc. As you walk from the exam room you feel confident that you have given the best performance that you could have done.

In the actual exam, if you find yourself panicking, the best remedy is to stop writing for a few moments and try to control your breathing. Under stress we tend to take fast, shallow breaths that can eventually produce dizziness. If you begin to panic, take a deep breath through your nose, filling your lungs. Let the breath out, and repeat the exercise several times. It won't take long, but it could relax you enough to stop the panic.

Read the questions

One very common mistake is to answer the first question you see that you know you can answer. Students often emerge blinking from the examination hall only to realise that there was a question on the paper they could have answered much more easily than the one they attempted. This is a horrible feeling. Don't let it happen to you. Skim through all the questions on the paper before deciding which ones you are going to focus on.

Handwriting

If you have to write your answers to an examination by hand, as most students still do, then your handwriting must be legible. This isn't a question of aesthetics; it needn't be beautiful or stylish. What matters is that someone else can read it without having to interpret what you probably wrote. Many of us rarely write at length by hand now, as word processing is increasingly common. So, if you know that your handwriting can be difficult to read, you should devote some time to making it more legible, perhaps by writing practice essays under strict time constraints.

Key points

- Exams are your chance to apply the basic principles of essay writing.
- The best way to avoid exam nerves is to prepare well.
- Use active rather than passive revision techniques.
- If you find yourself panicking in an exam, stop and take several deep breaths.
- Visualise a successful exam.
- Don't underestimate the part played by legible handwriting.

10
Improving your writing

Rewriting and editing

> ... often I completely change my mind in the course of writing an essay.
>
> (Susan Sontag, in Plimpton ed., 1999, p. 324)

In exams you won't have the luxury of rewriting what you have written. But with essays written in less pressured circumstances the best way to improve the finished result is to edit and, if necessary, rewrite it. In the age of word processing, editing has become a much more straightforward process than it was thirty years ago. Here is a checklist of questions that you might want to consult before handing in any essay:

Checklist

- Have I answered the question set?
- Have I made a case for a clearly stated conclusion?
- Have I used evidence, quotation and argument to make my case?
- Have I considered and answered possible counterarguments?
- Is the structure of my essay clearly signposted throughout?
- Have I acknowledged the sources of any quotations I've used?
- Have I provided a bibliography in the appropriate form?
- Is the tone of my essay appropriate for an academic context?
- Have I resorted to clichés or colloquialisms?
- Have I used long sentences that would be better split?
- Are there any adjectives or adverbs that I could remove?
- Is every paragraph relevant to the main argument of the essay?
- Have I made any slips in my use of apostrophes, commas or quotation marks?

- Have I spelt names of authors, places, books, etc. correctly?
- Is my writing legible?

Learn from feedback

Many students are more concerned with the mark they get than with the feedback tutors offer them. This is a foolish approach: the most valuable aspect of feedback is likely to be the specific comments you get on your work. If you ignore them, you will be lucky to improve on the mark you get for your first essay. Highlight or copy comments which seem particularly apt or useful. The most useful feedback is the kind that transfers to other essays. So, if a tutor points out that you haven't considered counterarguments to your position, think about whether this is an approach that is unique to the particular essay you have written, or a pattern in your work. If the latter, then you have a very clear guideline about where you should be putting in most effort, both in writing and particularly in rewriting or editing your work.

Learn from other students' essays

If you can persuade your friends to hand over their essays with their marks and comments, you will learn a great deal. Even if your friends' essays are not particularly well written and miss most of the important points, you can still learn from them: you might get a sense of where your own strengths and weaknesses lie, your friends might include points that you failed to make, or they might be strong in an area in which you are comparatively weak. At the very least you get a sense of what it is like as a marker to read someone else's essay, how difficult it can be to unravel bad handwriting, how irritating basic errors of grammar, spelling and punctuation can be.

Eliminate bad habits

As important as the cultivation of good habits is the elimination of bad ones. Remember that if you keep practising what you have always done in the past, you will probably only get good at doing what you have done in the past. To make progress you need to identify your good and bad habits, eliminate the bad ones and play to your strengths.

In order to help you eliminate bad habits and reinforce good ones I've sketched several character-types of poor essay writers below. My examples are almost caricatures, and most weak essay writers don't always fall neatly into one category or another, but the bad tendencies I've outlined *are* very common among students. If you recognise some of these bad tendencies in yourself, then that self-awareness should be the starting point for significant improvement. If you don't know what you are doing wrong, you will have difficulty moving forwards.

Do you recognise yourself here?

The alluder

The alluder is someone who makes allusions, oblique references to points rather than the points themselves. Alluders don't feel the need to spell out what they mean, they know that the marker of their essay understands the topic very well, and will only require the mention of a point to recognise the brilliance of the alluder's mind. Why bother explaining what a thinker thought when the marker knows all this already? Better surely simply to hint at ideas. Or so the alluder thinks.

The alluder's essay often degenerates into a kind of name-dropping with hints at the arguments that it would be tedious for the writer to spell out in detail. Alluders are often surprised by the low marks that they receive for their essays as they know much of the relevant material and feel that they have done enough to demonstrate this to the marker or examiner.

Most likely to write: 'Arthur Marwick elucidated the dominant ideas of the 1950s in his book about post-war Britain. He was mostly right in his analysis.'

Instead of: 'Arthur Marwick proposed sex and class as the two main themes running through 1950s popular culture, as typified by the novel and subsequent film of John Braine's *Room at the Top*. Although his selection of "typical" 1950s popular culture is to a degree subjective, it is certainly true that these themes recur and are foregrounded in many of the most successful and lasting novels and movies of that period.'

The fact regurgitator

The fact regurgitator has a good memory for detail and simply replays facts, whether relevant or not, at the slightest stimulus. This type of essay writer puts down everything he or she knows that is vaguely related to the topic. The result is usually barely readable and never gets to grips with the question asked.

Most likely to write (in response to a question about Rousseau's concept of the social contract): 'Jean-Jacques Rousseau, who ran away from Geneva in his early youth, and became one of the most controversial freelance writers of his age, despite admitting to being a flasher and a masochist in his posthumously published *Confessions* (not to mention having a public tiff with the great philosopher David Hume), was a moral philosopher of wide fame, though he was even more famous in his lifetime as a novelist.'

Instead of: 'Jean-Jacques Rousseau's notion of a social contract is based on his belief that in a so-called "state of nature", i.e. outside of any civilised common society, traits of the noble savage could emerge. He opens his book *The Social Contract* with the declaration that man is "born free, yet is everywhere in chains" . . .'

The digressor

Digressors, who may also be fact regurgitators, often begin their essays well with direct references to the question set, and so on. Some way into an example or illustration of a point, however, we find that they have temporary amnesia about why they are writing. The richness of the example takes over, and the digressors' essays become unfocused. Any topic loosely related to the one under discussion may find its way in. The conclusion of a digressor's essay typically feels tacked on the end, if it is there at all, as a non sequitur, something that does not follow logically from what has gone before.

Most likely to write (in response to 'Is Othello simply duped by Iago in Shakespeare's *Othello?*'): 'Throughout the play, Iago schemes to dupe Othello into believing that Desdemona, his wife, has been unfaithful to him. This is most obvious in the incident in which Iago contrives to have Othello see Cassio with a handkerchief that Othello had given Desdemona. This is reminiscent of the well-attested psychological tendency we all have to see what we expect to see: the idea that our "mental set", our expectations, actually affects what we do perceive. When someone writes "Paris in the the Spring" many of us will fail to read the second "the" because, expecting to see only one, we actually do see only one. This may be the basis of many optical illusions. It certainly is the source of so-called "*trompe l'oeil*" pictures – those that trick us that we are looking at a real thing (e.g. an envelope on a writing desk) rather than a painting of an envelope.'

Instead of: 'Throughout the play, Iago schemes to dupe Othello into believing that Desdemona, his wife, has been unfaithful to him. This is most obvious in the incident in which Iago contrives to have Othello see Cassio with a handkerchief that Othello had given Desdemona (ref.). There are, nevertheless, several key points during the play when Othello could easily have sought corroboration for Iago's insinuations. For example . . .'

The fence sitter

The fence sitter may know the topic very well and give excellent summaries of the important and relevant points. But even if asked a direct question, the fence sitter is likely just to present what can be said on either side of the issue, and never reach a forceful conclusion. The usual conclusion of a fence sitter's essay can be paraphrased as 'There are arguments on both sides.' What the fence sitter fails to realise is that part of what the question setter is trying to get the essay writer to do is weigh the competing arguments and come to a conclusion, not simply to list the arguments. On some occasions, of course, the arguments on either side of a question may be very well balanced. But this is not always the case. The fence sitter usually comes across as lacking the confidence to make a case for a conclusion.

Most likely to write (in response to 'Should fox hunting be banned?'): 'The arguments on both sides of the fox hunting debate are strong and complex. Given the weight of evidence that hunted foxes suffer great psychological and physical stress and pain, it might seem that the balance is strongly tipped towards maintaining a ban on hunting. Yet there are powerful arguments on the other side too. For instance, foxes cause a great deal of damage and need to be culled, and fox hunting does keep fox numbers down effectively. So, there are arguments on both sides.'

Instead of: 'As I have shown, the arguments for a ban on fox hunting far outweigh those on the other side. So, in answer to the question, yes, fox hunting should certainly be banned (and already is under United Kingdom law).'

Or, perhaps: 'Despite the arguments about the barbarity of fox hunting and its alleged effects on the fox, there are very strong arguments against an outright ban. The difficulty facing anyone wanting to preserve an absolute ban on fox hunting is that almost all the animal welfare arguments used to support it, if used in the context of farming in general, would require the government to ban all factory farming, and most transportation of mammals to slaughter-houses. Consequently, fox hunting should not be banned unless factory farming is banned, though there are very good reasons for monitoring it and minimising the worst practices involved in it.'

The summariser

The summariser is someone who methodically converts books, articles, lecture notes, and so on into shorter, often well-expressed, summaries. The sources of ideas are usually immediately recognisable, and there is no sense that the summariser has made the arguments and thoughts his or her own. Like the fence sitter, the summariser rarely comes to a conclusion, and if he or she does, it is usually someone else's conclusion summarised. The marker of a summariser is usually struck by how little the essay writer has thought about the subject matter. Clear summary is an important aspect of academic writing, but it should not be at the expense of the student making a case, weighing the evidence and drawing a conclusion.

Comment: The dangers of over-summarising only become apparent over the course of an essay when it emerges that the writer has failed to build a case or draw a conclusion, but has instead summarised (or even presented summaries of other people's summaries) throughout.

The personaliser

The personaliser's essay is immediately recognisable because of the frequency with which phrases such as 'I think', 'in my opinion', 'in my experience' and just 'I' occur. Sometimes these could simply be eliminated, since it is obvious that the essay is the opinion of the writer, and rather tedious to have this spelt out. This repetition of 'I' is inappropriate for most academic essays: each use is either unnecessary, or else suggests that the writer is incapable of decentring from his or her own experience to make a more objective assement of the issue being discussed. Worse still, typically a personaliser will argue from a single case – his or her own – without acknowledging that this experience may not be representative of the wider population or group under consideration. The personaliser may also significantly overrate the marker's interest in the essay writer's psychology, autobiography and opinions. The result is a confessional tone that suggests that the writer is not fully aware of the conventions and expectations of this kind of academic writing.

Most likely to write (in response to 'What are the main causes of the high incidence of obesity among children in Britain today?'): 'In my opinion, the main causes of obesity in Britain are that parents don't take time to teach their children about healthy eating; I also believe very strongly that school dinners are full of fat. My own experience confirms these two facts. My parents never taught me that there was anything wrong with eating large quantities of crisps and chips, and my school meals (which, believe me, were disgusting, but we were made to eat them nevertheless) usually consisted of fatty meat cooked in fatty gravy, followed by a sickly dessert. Personally, I think these two factors are the most important.'

Instead of: 'There are several important causes of childhood obesity in contemporary Britain. First, fast food with high fat content is readily available and heavily advertised to children. The huge growth in fast food outlets in inner cities since the 1970s coincides with significant increases in childhood obesity. Fast food outlets target children: for example, burger chains often advertise free toys as a way of enticing children to persuade their parents to buy this fast food. Second, many children are ignorant of the health risks of a diet high in fatty food. Third, many school meals are high in fat content. When children opt to bring sandwiches, their parents frequently include crisps and other fatty snacks in their lunchboxes.'

The asserter

The asserter doesn't feel the need to justify anything he or she writes. An asserter's essay is typically just a list of opinions and bold pronouncements. The asserter completely misses the point of essay writing, which is to demonstrate an understanding of the subject matter and an ability to think clearly about it. Those marking essays are quickly exasperated by reading a series of conclusions with no argument or evidence leading to those conclusions.

Most likely to write (in response to 'Critically discuss Freud's theory of psychoanalysis.'): 'Freud was misguided. His idea that we have an unconscious mind that affects our everyday life is simply wrong-headed. His belief that the unconscious manifests itself through dreams and so-called "Freudian slips" is clearly absurd. Therefore, there is nothing to be said in favour of the Freudian theory of psychoanalysis.'

Instead of, for example: 'Freud's theory of psychoanalysis included the claim that unconscious forces have a significant impact on all our lives. One criticism of this claim is that it is impossible to dis-prove it. If you deny that the Freudian unconscious exists, Freudians will claim that you are simply providing evidence that it *does* exist: it is your unconscious that is making you so aggressively resistant to believing in the unconscious.'

The jargonist

The jargonist revels in being difficult to understand. Give a jargonist a new term and he or she will happily use it several times in a sentence. The more obscure the term, the better. The jargonist believes that technical language makes his or her essay sound more learned. In truth, excessive use of jargon is frequently a smokescreen to hide the depths of a writer's ignorance. As the contemporary philosopher John Searle has wisely pointed out, 'If you can't say it clearly, you haven't understood it yourself.'

Most likely to write (in response to 'How plausible is the idea that the world bears evidence of God as its creator?'): 'The teleological argument from a posteriori evidence, more than *a priori*, cosmological arguments, has *prima facie* plausibility, yet, *ipso facto*, should be viewed with suspicion. The fallacious analogical structure of reasoning, and dubious epistemological assumptions, albeit based on empirical observations, lend themselves to refutation.'

Instead of: 'The design argument is based on the idea that, for example, the sophistication of the human eye can only adequately be explained by the existence of a Divine Designer (i.e. God) who conceived of and created this complex and highly effective organ. Darwin's alternative explanation of how organisms adapt and evolve through a process of natural selection to some degree undermines this style of argument.'

The bullet pointer

The bullet pointer's essays frequently degenerate into lists of ungrammatical sentences. Although the content of the essay may be good, the bullet pointer doesn't take the trouble to abide by the convention of writing coherent prose. At its worst, this bullet pointing can be superficial in content as well as lazy as prose.

Most likely to write (in response to '"In Thomas Hardy's *The Mayor of Casterbridge* the hero is entirely responsible for his own downfall." Discuss.'):

- 'The Mayor of Casterbridge sold his wife at an auction, so initiated events that came back to cause his downfall.

- But Hardy frequently alludes to Fate in the novel.
- Yet there are several points in the novel where the Mayor allowed his rivalry with Farfrae to obscure his judgement.
- Therefore the quotation in the question is correct.'

Instead of: 'Hardy makes clear in the novel that the Mayor of Casterbridge's early drunken decision to auction his own wife was the factor that triggered a series of events that eventually culminate in his downfall. Fate played its part, but the initial descent was begun by the Mayor's own foolish act . . .'

The copy-and-paster

The copy-and-paster doesn't believe in wasting anything. Bits of other essays, unattributed quotations and indeed anything that more or less fits into the essay are likely to appear, hoisted into place using the copy and paste commands on a word processor. The mixture of styles, tenses, subject matter – and sometimes even fonts – quickly give the copy-and-paster away. Essays produced by such extreme and lazy methods of collage are seldom any good. There is a real danger of plagiarism, too, if copy-and-pasters are careless about attributing the sources of the words that they so freely cut and paste (see 'The plagiarist' below).

Most likely to write: 'The copy-and-paster doesn't believe in wasting anything. Bits of other essays, unattributed quotations, and indeed anything that more or less fits into the essay are likely to appear, hoisted into place using the copy and paste commands on a word processor.'

The colloquialist

The colloquialist has no idea about the appropriate tone for academic essay writing. He or she deliberately interjects jokey asides and colloquial language at every imaginable opportunity. The colloquialist's essay is usually peppered with clichés. The result can be extremely irritating.

Most likely to write (in response to 'What were the main causes of the First World War?'): 'At the end of the day, the First World War was the last century's biggest fiasco. A real mudbath, with the generals making a dog's dinner of the tactics and bottling some serious decisions. You may well ask what caused this pig's ear of a war. There were several dodgy things going on at the time . . .'

Instead of: 'There were three principal causes of the First World War: . . .'

The plagiarist

The plagiarist takes from other writers and doesn't bother to acknowledge his or her sources. Passing others' work off as your own is a very serious offence in most academic contexts. The plagiarist often does this inadvertently, through sloppy notetaking rather than malice. But the authorities may not believe this, taking it as an excuse. Plagiarism comes in degrees. At its worst it is straightforward deception.

Most likely to write (in response to 'What is plagiarism?'): 'The plagiarist takes from other writers and doesn't bother to acknowledge his or her sources. Passing others' work off as your own is a very serious offence in most academic contexts. The plagiarist often does this inadvertently, through sloppy notetaking rather than malice.'

Instead of: 'In *The Basics of Essay Writing,* Nigel Warburton describes the plagiarist as someone who 'takes from other writers and doesn't bother to acknowledge his or her sources' (Warburton, 2005, p. 107).'

Key points

- Improve your essay by editing and, if necessary, rewriting it.
- Use the checklist provided on pages 95–6 to help you identify areas needing attention at the editing stage.
- Take feedback seriously.
- Identify and eliminate bad habits; reinforce good ones.

Conclusion

Good luck

The basics of essay writing aren't complicated. They are quite straightforward to learn. If you form good habits in this area, you can make significant improvements very quickly. Every essay that you write should be another opportunity to develop your skills and to put the principles covered in this book into practice.

Good luck with your writing.

If you have found this book useful, or have any thoughts about how I might improve it in future editions, please email me at n.warburton@open.ac.uk.

Website: http://www.nigelwarburton.com

Bibliography and
further reading

Bibliography

Berra, Yogi (1998) *The Yogi Book*, New York: Workman Publishing.

Brande, Dorothea (1983) *Becoming a Writer*, London: Macmillan.

Dixon, Thomas (2004) *How to Get a First*, London: Routledge.

Evans, Harold (2000) *Essential English for Journalists, Editors and Writers*, revised edition, London: Pimlico.

Goldberg, Natalie (1998) *Writing Down the Bones*, Boston: Shambhala.

Gowers, Ernest [3rd edition revised by Sidney Greenbaum and Janet Whitcut] (1987) *The Complete Plain Words*, London: Penguin.

Law, Stephen (2003) *The Philosophy Gym*, London: Review.

Plimpton, George, ed. (1999) *Women Writers at Work*, London: Harvill.

Strunk, William Jr and White, E. B. (2000) *The Elements of Style*, 4th edition, Boston, MA: Allyn and Bacon.

Warburton, Nigel (2004) *Philosophy: The Essential Study Guide*, London: Routledge.

Further reading

I've listed several books for further reading below. I wouldn't recommend spending too long reading about essay writing: as I stressed in my introduction, to improve in this area you need to practise.

Writing well

Strunk, William Jr and White, E. B. (2000) *The Elements of Style*, 4th edition, Boston, MA: Allyn and Bacon.

Study skills

Chambers, Ellie and Northedge, Andrew (1997) *The Arts Good Study Guide*, Milton Keynes: The Open University.

Punctuation

Truss, Lynne (2003) *Eats, Shoots and Leaves*, London: Profile.

Making a case

Weston, Anthony (2001) *A Rulebook for Argument*, 3rd edition, Indianapolis: Hackett.

Critical thinking

Warburton, Nigel (2000) *Thinking from A to Z*, 2nd edition, London: Routledge.

Note-taking

Buzan, Tony and Buzan, Barry (2003) *The Mind Map Book*, revised edition, London: BBC Worldwide.

Internet resources

There are numerous websites devoted to essay writing. Many of these are linked to colleges and universities. Not all the advice available online is useful, so you will need to read anything there with a critical eye. Also, be wary of the trap of spending hours surfing the Internet as a way of avoiding the activity of writing.

Bibliography and further reading

The Open University short course A173 *Start Writing Essays* is taught online. Further details of this course can be found at www.open.ac.uk, call 01908 653231 or email general-enquiries@ open.ac.uk.

Lightning Source UK Ltd.
Milton Keynes UK
UKOW02n2149020616

275488UK00007B/28/P